CYNTHIA WILLEY MRSC is a
chemistry in sixth form colleges ɛ
and Member of the Royal Socie
more than a decade ago after twɛ
still actively involved in the education system, currently supporting
Wildern School as an exam invigilator. As well as being a keen
creative writer, Cynthia is a voluntary worker at Manor Farm
Country Park.

Cynthia currently lives with her husband Alan in Hedge End,
Southampton.

It Wasn't Me, Miss

CYNTHIA WILLEY

SilverWood

Published in 2017 by SilverWood Books

SilverWood Books Ltd
14 Small Street, Bristol, BS1 1DE, United Kingdom
www.silverwoodbooks.co.uk

ISBN 978-1-78132-606-0 (paperback)
ISBN 978-1-78132-607-7 (ebook)

British Library Cataloguing in Publication Data
A CIP catalogue record for this book is available from
the British Library

Page design and typesetting by SilverWood Books
Printed on responsibly sourced paper

I dedicate this book to my sons Ian and Stephen

PREFACE

I spent twenty-eight years teaching science and chemistry, mainly to students in sixth-form colleges. I also spent a short while in two schools. I loved it, and there was never a dull moment. Before teaching I worked for three years; first in a chemistry laboratory and secondly in a biochemistry laboratory in a research facility. However, from a very young age I knew I wanted to teach. So I studied for my teaching diploma, which included working in a college for a term. My first story is taken from this teaching practice. In at the deep end!

This collection of stories is a treasury of my memories of those twenty-eight years. If any of them ring a bell, remember you're not alone. I hope these stories show you that when something goes wrong it's not always your fault. Students can do daft things and you can't always predict what mistakes they will make. But it'll be all right in the end. Just laugh about it and remember you're doing your best, and you're only human after all.

A SPEEDY EVACUATION

I tell one of the female students, "Don't worry, breathe deeply and you'll be fine. At least it's warm and sunny out here on the grass and not like last week when it was snowing." But I'm shivering myself. It hadn't been a difficult experiment to set up, although – particularly in terms of health and safety – it did require a certain degree of common sense. The trouble is, this is often lacking in many students, despite the fact that they are eighteen years old and have studied chemistry at school for two years already.

Half an hour before, I had been sitting in the staff room having a nice cup of tea, and chatting to the chemistry lecturer at the college where I was completing my teaching practice. The classes were going very well and my confidence was growing. He had asked me if I was ready for this particular practical and I said yes, although I was quite nervous because of the safety issue. We decided he would sit at the back of the classroom just for support.

The practical involved making an organic compound, which required using the method of refluxing. This is a distillation technique using the condensation of vapours and the return of them back to the system. I gave the students a handout with a diagram on it, and detailed instructions of how to put the apparatus together correctly. I emphasised to them that the most important thing to remember about this technique was that the water from the tap must go in at the bottom of the connecting tube and out at the top into the sink. If this is not done and it's connected the other way around then fumes, often dangerous ones, will be released into the room. And of course they must remember to turn on the tap.

When they were all ready to start, I went around each pair of students to check that indeed they had connected up all the apparatus correctly. We were all set to go so they turned on the Bunsens and waited for the reaction to start.

It all seemed to be going well and I wondered what on Earth I had been worrying about. Then suddenly I started to cough and I noticed that some of the students were coughing as well. At first I thought they were being silly, but then I saw white fumes coming out of one of the sets of apparatus. The choking fumes began to get thicker and I started to panic. My mind was racing and I could see the newspaper headline: 'Twelve students, a lecturer and student lecturer rushed to hospital unconscious.' That would be the end of my career before it had even started!

I felt a tap on the shoulder and jumped. "Come on," said my tutor. "Let's get them out of here. Calmly though, don't rush – we don't want to panic them. Assemble them on the grass." Good job he was calm. Mind you, he had years of experience behind him and I was just starting out.

Fortunately for us, the chemistry laboratory was at the end of a corridor which led directly out on to the fields, so no harm was done. We learnt afterwards that the smell had permeated around the college, but no-one took much notice as it was assumed it was only the chemists making nasty smells again!

What on Earth had happened? It turned out that one of the pairs had thought that once the condenser was full of water, they could turn the tap off. They thought it would save water if it wasn't running all the time. But they hadn't realised that the condenser would automatically empty of water. Hopefully, it's a lesson they won't forget. Since then I have emphasised the importance of running water in these experiments.

AN INTERESTING EXPERIMENT

"Come on, hurry up, George! You're late! We arranged to meet fifteen minutes ago. You said you'd pick up your bike from the sheds and meet me here at the gate."

"All right, don't go on, Peter. I couldn't get here any earlier, all right? My class didn't finish until 10.30."

"So why didn't you just say you had a dentist appointment and had to leave early? You usually do that all the time."

"Because this time we were doing a practical, and for once I was quite enjoying it. Okay?"

"George, you look red in the face and a bit odd."

"Thanks for that."

"Why isn't Bill with you?"

"Well, he's not in my class is he? Perhaps he bunked off. I don't know where he is. He wasn't at the bike sheds so I thought he was with you."

"Actually, George, I thought you had been banned from attending any classes."

"I have, all except GCSE science. My teacher said she would allow me to stay in the class. Apparently she's determined I'll pass this GCSE whether I like it or not. I can't argue with that, can I?"

"I suppose not. Although what you're going to do with just one

GCSE I can't imagine. Anyway, what was this practical that was so interesting you couldn't leave?"

"We were making an organic ester."

"A what?"

"Well, it's a bit like making salt. Do you remember the experiment last year when we mixed an acid and a base to make salt?"

"Not really. But then I hated science."

"Well, you add alcohol to a type of organic acid, carbox… carboxyl…carboxylic acid, that's it."

"Have you swallowed a chemistry book?"

"Very funny. It was interesting. I think even you might have enjoyed it. We used alcohol in a burette."

"Alcohol? What, like vodka or gin?"

"No, ethanol, dickhead. Now you're going to tell me you can't remember what a burette is."

"Yes, you're right. What is it?"

"It's a long thin measuring tube with a tap at the bottom of it."

"Really? I don't remember using one of them."

"That's probably because you bunked off school so often. Anyway, do you want to hear why it was so interesting or not?"

"Might as well while we're waiting for Bill."

"We placed acetic acid, colourless vinegar to you, in a flask with an indicator. We ran in the alcohol from the burette, which was clamped above it. When the colour changes an ester has been formed."

"I think that alcohol's gone to your head."

"The lab smelled lovely."

"What sort of acid was it, speed?"

"Don't be stupid."

"Here's Bill now. Hi! You're late!"

"Blimey, George, you look pissed. I watched you cycling over the field and it definitely looked as if you had had one over the eight. In fact, I saw your whole class come out and they all seemed worse for wear. What on Earth were you doing in your class?"

"Get this, he was making an ester from alcohol and an acid."

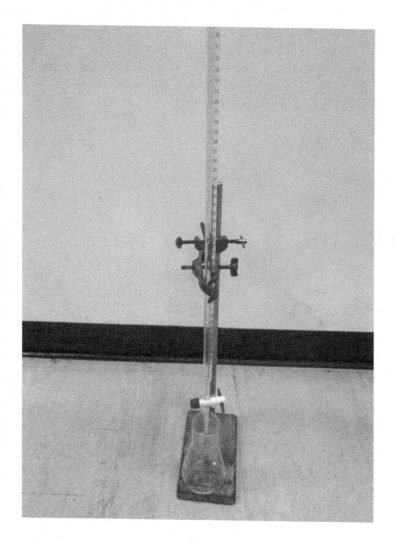

"Wow! I wish I'd been there. I was stuck in a physics class being bored to death by a talk on relativity."

"Relative what? You sound like him. Have you swallowed a physics book? Right, let's go."

"Wow, George, you do look a bit wobbly on that bike. Will you be okay on the road?"

"Of course I will. I haven't been drinking the alcohol, have I?"

"Well, we had better look out for the Old Bill. We don't want you failing a breath test, do we now? What do you think, Peter?"

"Well, they certainly won't believe that you're like this because you've been doing a science experiment."

A DRAMA IN A COSMETIC SCIENCE CLASS

I'm sitting here waiting for the students to come in and mulling over last week's disastrous lesson. I must have been mad to volunteer to run this cosmetic science link course. I would never have thought that, at the age of fifteen, these girls' ability in reading and writing would be so poor, and that after the first lesson I would have to rewrite all the handouts. It was apparent that most of them were unable to recognise words of more than four syllables and certainly, sentences of more than four or five words they found very difficult. Where our intonation would drop at the end of a sentence, theirs did not. They were simply reading one word at a time without really understanding what they were reading.

I find this very sad. I'm sure that when they entered secondary education at the age of eleven they were able to read. So what happened in their years at secondary school? These girls are all school truants and as such have missed a lot of basic education. They also have a lot of behavioural issues. Here they come.

"Come on now, get yourself a lab coat and settle down! Now, I have prepared some better handouts for you this week. You're going to make hand cream and you can take it home." I'm thinking to myself that they must be able to follow these instructions. The method is a series of numbered steps, and the first instruction is to collect a specific size of beaker from the front bench! They seem to be coping very well and are busy carrying out the first steps in making the cream.

Suddenly the door flies open and a latecomer comes crashing in.

"Sorry I'm late." She scowls.

"Okay, grab a coat and sit down. Right. I'll briefly go through the handout with you." She seems agitated and spoiling for a fight. Suddenly she shouts at me.

"This is boring. We're only here because we have to be." This latecomer is becoming very confrontational. I must try to calm her down. I'm having mixed emotions. After further lip I find myself becoming angry. She seems to be trying to alienate the group against me. Suddenly I put my hands on a stool in front of me and I simply have this urge to pick it up and hit her with it. Fortunately, I come to my senses. What am I thinking? I put it down and rush out of the room, still shaking, and bump into the maths teacher from over the way.

"What's the matter?"

"Can you remove one of the girls from my class before I hit her?"

"Of course! Where is she?"

"In here." He comes back with me and sends her away.

"You carry on with your class and tell me all about it at tea."

"Okay." The rest of the class carry on working and the girls are really pleased with their cream once they've made it. They can't wait to take it home to show their friends and try it out.

At the bell I make my way to the refectory.

"I've got you a cup of tea. Now tell me what happened in there."

"I'm feeling a bit down over this incident and the fact that she made me so angry."

To cheer me up he tells me of an incident with a student on another link course. It was a maths lesson and he was writing on the board when a real metal dart came flying past his ear and hit the blackboard with a thud. He picked the boy who had thrown it up by the scruff of his neck and threw him out. The boy was kicked off the course and out of the college. You wouldn't think that colleges could be such dangerous places! Mind you at least in those days you could do something about these students. Nowadays you would have to fill out endless forms in triplicate, have the parents in to be told that it was probably your fault he did it, and be charged with assault for throwing him out. How times have changed!

I dreaded the following week but it appeared the students were all on my side. Apart from the problem girl they all turned up in their half term. I like to think I made a difference.

A DIFFICULT LESSON

I keep looking at the door. They will be here in a minute. Now, have I got everything? Yes. My notes, which are meticulous, and all the overhead transparencies are very clear and precise. I did think about using a magnet board but I quickly dismissed that idea. The students do like using it but I think it could cause chaos with this topic. I'm not sure how I'm going to cope. They can probably teach me a thing or two. The door opens and I look at my watch. It's too early. They can't be that keen, surely?

"Oh, hi, Frank. What can I do for you?"

"Well, I came to give you a few words of support. I know you don't really like teaching biology, but, unfortunately, being new to the college, I had to put it on your timetable. Sorry."

"That's okay. I know you had no choice. Most of the topics in the syllabus are fine – it's just this one."

"Yes, I can understand that. Sixteen-year-old hormonal boys are not the easiest to teach at the best of times. But this topic, well, that's why I came to see you were okay and see if you need any help, and wish you luck. But I can see you're well prepared. I think not using the magnet board was very wise."

"Yes, can you imagine, Frank, the resulting chaos sticking magnets on a very large chart? I have had a brilliant idea, though.

There's one boy in the class, very likeable, but also very mouthy."

"I know the one you mean."

"Well, my idea revolves around him."

"Okay, let me know how it goes. Good luck."

The door opens and they all push past Frank as he leaves.

"Hi, miss, we're really looking forward to this lesson."

"I expect you are. Come on, quieten down and get your books out."

I can feel their eyes on me in anticipation and can feel them getting ready to give me a hard time. But I keep my nerve. I look directly at this boy.

"Now, I'm sure that you know all about sexual reproduction, so perhaps you would like to tell the class how babies are conceived."

He is stunned, as are the rest of the class. He shifts in his chair. I look around the room and they're all sitting in complete silence looking down at their books. This is the quietest they have ever been. Not even a titter. I've cracked it. I deliver my lesson and none of them even attempts to ask a question.

Now there is just the class on contraception and venereal diseases to cope with!

BEYOND BELIEF

I'm sitting here having a sip of my tea and eating a biscuit to calm me down. My hands are still shaking as I can't believe what has just happened. Ten years in teaching is a long time, but perhaps you get blasé after a while and you forget you're dealing with potentially dangerous chemicals. These can be potent or even lethal. So what happened? I'll tell you.

I arrived at work early as usual and it was a lovely sunny day. It was 8.30 and I was getting the lesson ready for my GNVQ intermediate science class. The students are lovely – not particularly academic, but they are ready and willing to learn, as most of them want to go on to study chemistry at university if they can. The lesson lasts an hour and a half, so we have theory first, followed by a small practical. This keeps their interest.

Before they arrived I checked that all of the chemicals and apparatus had been set out ready by the technician. And today was no different. The topic was how to identify the metal part of a compound (for example, potassium and sodium ions) using flame tests. Very simply, small samples of compounds of these metals are placed on a watch glass and a few drops of concentrated hydrochloric acid are placed on the crystals. Then a nichrome wire is dipped in the mixture and placed in the flame of a Bunsen burner. The students would see different coloured flames corresponding to the different metal ions. Simple enough, and I had taught this lesson more times than I care to remember.

So the students put on their lab coats and collected the relevant apparatus. Now there were eighteen students in the class and they were working in pairs, so there were nine watch glasses between the six benches. One of the pair put a sample of potassium chloride on a watch glass with a few drops of concentrated acid using a teat pipette, and the other lit the Bunsen. I made sure that they only used a couple of drops of the acid for each one and that they had their safety spectacles on.

All of a sudden I became aware of a really pungent choking smell and a green coloured vapour rising from the watch glasses. Some of the students began to cough so I immediately evacuated the laboratory, having turned the Bunsens off and opened the windows. I sent the students off to the refectory for their break and went back in the lab to see what on Earth had happened. I couldn't understand it.

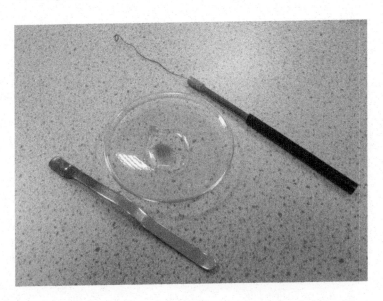

But then I looked at the bottle of potassium chloride, and was horrified to find that the label said 'potassium chlorate'. How could I have missed it? I couldn't really blame the lab technician as I should have double-checked it myself. It was beyond belief that such a very reliable technician could make such a mistake, and even worse that I didn't spot it.

Now you may wonder what the difference is between chloride and chlorate. The answer is: a massive one! Potassium chlorate and concentrated hydrochloric acid combine to form chlorine gas. This gas is extremely poisonous – it was used successfully as a weapon in the First World War, hence the use of gas masks in the trenches. So, as I said earlier, you can't assume anything when dealing with chemicals. I certainly won't do that again! But don't worry; the students were completely unharmed, and in fact enjoyed their extended tea break.

SICK IN GERMANY

I am looking forward to this trip with my students to Germany. There are three of us adults this year. With me is a male colleague and a friend of mine, Dorothy, who speaks German as I do. We're all staying in a nice small hotel in the village.

"I had better set the alarm for 7.30," I say in our room on the first evening.

"How long is the journey going to be?" my friend asks me.

"We're catching the first train at 9.00 but we have to walk to the station, and you know how fast students walk."

"Yes, snail's pace!"

"There will be two changes but we'll be met by our guide for the day in a company bus. It should be really interesting."

"It had better be after all the travelling!"

"I do hope they take my advice about going to sleep early for tonight."

"You're being optimistic, aren't you?"

"Yes, probably."

"Are you going to write up your diary?"

"Yes. It'll only be a short paragraph. I'll have to report back," I lie back, thinking about the following day. It's a bit ambitious, but I'm sure it'll be worth it. I switch off the light.

Suddenly I'm aware of someone banging on our bedroom door.

"What on Earth? What time is it?" I glance at the tiny alarm clock beside my bed. My friend is fast asleep, or so I think. She quickly sits up.

"What's the matter?" she asks.

"Someone's at the door."

"Shall I go?"

"No, it's okay. I will."

As I open the door there are two panicky faces staring at me. "Miss, miss. One of the boys has been sick on the bedroom floor."

"Really? Why didn't you knock on sir's door? He's right next to you. Instead you climb two flights of stairs to wake me up!"

"Oh, but, miss, we thought you would be more sympathetic."

"Really? Well, you know what thought did, don't you?" I reply grumpily.

"Please, miss, he's looking very pale and we don't know what to do."

"All right. I'll come down."

"Shall I come and help you?" my friend asks.

"No, you're all right. I'll handle it. Go back to bed." I put my dressing gown on, thinking it's a good job I have a thick nightdress on, and follow the boys downstairs.

I stop at sir's door and knock loudly. The door opens slightly and he peers around the small gap. Bleary-eyed, he looks at me quizzically. "What's up?"

"You must sleep like a log. Didn't you hear the noise next door?"

"No, I didn't."

"Well, get your dressing gown on. I need a chaperone to go into a boy's bedroom."

As I wait for him to make himself respectable, I moan out loud so he can hear: "I told them to go to bed early as we're visiting the hydroelectric power station in Luxembourg tomorrow, and it'll be a very long and tiring journey. I might as well have been talking to a brick wall for all the notice they've taken of my advice."

We go into the boy's room. "Where is he then?"

"In the bathroom, miss." I open the door to see him wrapped around the toilet seat.

"So! Despite my warning, you've all been drinking, and by the looks of him, far too much."

"No! He didn't drink too much, but we think he's not used to it."

"Give us a hand and get him into bed. I'll put a large plastic bag next to him, although I think he'll sleep soundly for the rest of the night. Clear up this mess and don't be late for breakfast or you'll go without. Goodnight." I leave the room and climb the stairs.

Back in my room, I jump into bed.

"Everything all right?" my friend asks.

"Yes, nothing a good night's sleep won't put right, but he'll have a bad head in the morning. It'll serve him right or, as they say in German, *Es geschiet ihn recht*!"

A DAWN RAID

I stand there in his office looking at my head of department. I'm speechless. He has the letter in his hand.

My mind shoots back to a week ago, sitting in a German cafe with my two colleagues.

"This is lovely. What a week we've had, and I think the students have enjoyed it. What do you think?" I said.

"Well, they have certainly enjoyed the social side of the visit. I personally am looking forward to going home tomorrow. I can't wait. You and your ideas about widening your students' horizons and opening their minds to new experiences! It certainly opened mine," my physics collegue said.

"Oh, come on! You enjoyed it."

"Have a free holiday, you said."

"You get nothing for nothing in this world."

"Don't I know it!"

"Come on, we visited a hydroelectric power station with a fabulous lunch afterwards, a winery with free wine, had a free breakfast at a school and a free lunch at the university. What more could you ask for? I was the one who drew the short straw, collecting water from the river in jam jars in the pouring rain."

"I suppose you're right. It has been an interesting week. I have

31

to admit we've eaten a lot. However, I'm glad we're going home tomorrow."

"About that. I hope the students leave the room clean and tidy. In the morning, while the coach is being loaded with their luggage, I'll go and check."

It was quite manic the following morning, but at least all the students were at breakfast and had finished packing.

"Right, you get them all on the bus and I'll check their rooms," I told my colleagues.

I jumped as I felt a hand on my shoulder. It was the lady who owned the guesthouse. She asked me to follow her. Her face was like thunder as she spoke to me in German. She said she had carried out *ein Überraschungsangriff*, and I needed to come with her immediately to one of the rooms. What on Earth is that? I thought, I must look it up in the German dictionary when I get a chance.

We went up to one of the rooms and she threw open the door.

"Look!" she shouted. "Your students did this." I stared disbelievingly at the wall behind the bed. It was pitted, as if someone had been stabbing it with a broom handle. Surely not, I thought, I know they are mischievous but this is pure vandalism! She started shouting again and I really didn't know what to say.

"I will be writing to your college to charge them for the damage."

I was at a loss. I felt sure that there was a mistake.

Back in the office of my head of department, he says: "This is the letter we were expecting, but don't worry, I'll deal with it. I believe she was trying it on and the damage was already there. I shall be writing to her to say so."

"Thank you." I leave his office and feel as if a weight has been lifted from my shoulders. I'm so pleased to see my colleague, who has been waiting outside. "It's okay. He will deal with it."

"Something I meant to ask you. What did she mean by *ein Überraschungsangriff*?" he asked.

"Oh, it's a dawn raid!"

WAITING TO HEAR

Poor old John! I bet he is bored out of his brain and here we are tucking into a large four-course lunch. I can't believe it. We're being treated like royalty, with lunch fit for a king and silver service as well. The students are very quiet, which is quite unusual for them. Normally you can't shut them up! I think they're not sure about the food, as it's definitely not what they're used to back home. But then most of them have never seen, let alone eaten, German food. And in such a posh setting. I, on the other hand, love it. I look over at my colleague Mary, who agrees that they are behaving very well.

"I hope John is okay. We still haven't heard from him. I know I gave him enough instructions and the phone number. It must have arrived, otherwise he would have rung this morning. Trouble is I can't ring him. It seemed quite straightforward when I arranged it – a nuisance, but not impossible. I really thought I had covered all the problem dates. But no! This particular student had wanted to come on the trip so I had to accommodate him."

"Yes, you had to," she says.

"The whole visit today has gone very well, don't you think? They've actually asked a few sensible questions. This was probably because earlier this week we visited the science laboratories at Goethe University. They had 'learnt' – I say that loosely – all about testing the gold content of jewellery. They were certainly interested in that! So this visit to Degussa-Hüls to see the precious metal extraction process had them enthralled."

"Yes, they certainly seemed to have enjoyed it."

Now on the coffee and biscuits, again I think about John. Well, he did volunteer and the student is a member of his class. I'm feeling quite full now and the students are starting to get a bit restless. I get out the college phone and look at it. John should be finished by now so I suppose I could ring him, but I really can't work this contraption. I was shown how to use it before we came away but I can't even remember how to dial out. This new-fangled technology! Suddenly the phone rings.

"Oh, for heaven's sake, what do I press?"

"There you are, miss," a student says, helping me.

"Thank you." I'm filled with trepidation and I don't know why. "Hello? Oh, it's you, John. How did it go? You've missed a fantastic lunch. Sorry!"

"Yes, it was fine. He wrote quite a lot but since I wasn't allowed to read it, I can't be sure. There was a slight panic at first as the paper only arrived this morning, half an hour before the start time," he says.

In future I think if a student has an official exam during a residential school trip then they shouldn't go on the trip. It would have been bad enough if we had been in England, but Germany!

HE DISAPPEARED INTO THE DARKNESS

I turn to my colleague who is sitting next to me on the coach. "How much longer until we get back to the college?" I ask. I never want to do this again. "You know, I was really looking forward to this week away with the students. It was a first, I had plenty of help, and they're not children. So what went wrong? After all, I speak the language and all the visits were mapped out and confirmed."

He sighs, "Trouble is they are teenagers, even if they are over seventeen, and they're a long way from home. You couldn't have done any more. The ungrateful bunch!"

It's getting dark. I check my watch again. Only about fifteen minutes now until we're back at the college.

"Are you going to check on them?" he asks.

"No, I don't think so. They are fairly quiet."

"That's the problem. What are they up to at the back, I wonder?"

"Don't care." I began to think back over the week. It really hadn't gone well from the start. The guesthouse, although backing directly onto a busy multi-railway line, had been in a quiet village and seemed very comfortable. I had used coaches before for day trips. I should have known better. The boat over from Dover ended up with one of the students being violently sick – alcohol-fuelled, of course. The rest of the journey that followed was a nightmare.

When we arrived at the guesthouse they rushed off to look at their rooms, the first and last time they weren't late.

Then one of them announced that they had lost £50 and asked what I was going to do about it. Apparently, it must have been stolen! One of the staff came up with the brilliant idea of searching all the bags and rooms. Surprise, surprise! The money appeared out of thin air.

I woke the first morning to a very loud rap on the door. It was the owner of the guesthouse who was complaining bitterly about the noise late into the night, which had disturbed the other guests, and also the state of their rooms. Bottles everywhere, so I was informed.

I convened a meeting with all of the students and read them the riot act. I made each one of them write a letter of apology. Of course they didn't mean it but at least they were much quieter with their drinking for the rest of the week. I also kept a close eye on their rooms. The trips out were always noisy and invariably there were always a few of them who were late no matter what I said. On reflection I should have just left them behind. However, they might have got into even more mischief! This college trip was turning into a nightmare.

I feel a nudge from my colleague. "What's that smell? Alcohol?"

"No, something else. I can't place it," I say.

"Marijuana, mate," the driver informs us.

"Thank you, I should have guessed," I say.

The colleague next to me says "They'll pay for this, don't you worry."

We stop and my colleague helps to unload the rucksacks from the coach. Some of the students are laughing, probably at us. Not one of them stops to say thanks for taking them on the trip. One in particular, who I think was handing out the weed, gives me a look to say 'you won't get me'. He jumps off the bus and with a laugh he disappears into the darkness.

"Don't worry, the joke will be on him. He'll be laughing on the other side of his face when he opens his bag," my colleague assures me.

"What do you mean?"

"What do you think happens when a soft rucksack filled with bottles of alcohol hits the hard concrete of the pavement with force?"

THE SCIENCE DEPARTMENT PANTOMIME

Christmas means it's pantomime time again, but this isn't the usual run-of-the-mill panto. This is one put on for the staff and students at the college by the members of the science department, where I work. We put one on every year to raise money for charity and the students love it. Let me introduce myself. I am Grumpy, one of the seven teenage mutant dwarf science lecturers. I've spent weeks rehearsing and learning my lines. Now I can hear the chatter in the lecture room as the students are eagerly awaiting the extravaganza.

I'm very nervous. I hope I don't forget my lines. I can hear the compere setting the scene and warning the audience that the scenes will contravene the sex discrimination act, the disability act and the abuse of students act, but they are not to worry as it's designed to offend everyone on a very personal level. Suddenly the chatter changes to roars of laughter as Luigi and Ricardo, who are the pantomime comedians, start their warm-up routine of climbing over the tiered seats to the pretty young students. They really are rude, you know, but the students love it. They take a rise out of all the staff with their language and innuendos.

The story, which is loosely based on the original Snow White, has now started and I'll be on in about fifteen minutes. Queen Phil, a maths lecturer, is the baddy who wants to get rid of Smee White.

He has been told by the mirror on the wall that she is now not only the fairest of them all, but the best mathematics lecturer of them all as well. She is very pretty with blue eyes and long soft golden hair, but she has lots of dandruff. The dwarves work in the science prep room. A meat pie from the canteen, rather than an apple, given to her by Queen Phil disguised as a hippy, is what poisons Smee White.

The other dwarves join me outside the lecture room. There are two of us in green and we're the serious ones Grumpy and Dumpy. The two chatterboxes, Stumpy and Frumpy, giggle all the time and are in pink. Bumpy and Lumpy, who are very athletic, are in orange. Now the seventh one, well don't ask. He's dressed in a grubby-looking mackintosh acting like a dirty old man and his name is Rumpy Pumpy. I said it was rude, didn't I? Although in his case, crude. He always gets lots of boos and hisses. We hear our cue and we're on. "High ho, hi ho, it's off to work we go," we sing with gusto.

Now normally if you're in the pantomime you escape being the butt of the comedian's jokes. They appear to have made an exception in my case. While we're all waiting for the final entrance, I hear them planning their escape from the wrath of Queen Phil. The handsome biology technician has managed to wake up Smee White from her sleep with a kiss.

"The best line of defence is attack," says Luigi.

"Yes," says Ricardo, "And I know the best person to use: Grumpy. She's known as the science department Rottweiler."

When I asked a group of students recently in the student union whether they preferred to be bitten by a Rottweiler or me, they said the Rottweiler! Harsh but fair. So my character is quite apt. You get harangued even if you're in the pantomime. And here I am making a fool of myself alongside all the other members of the cast. Still, teaching is like acting anyway.

At the end, as in a usual pantomime, the whole cast joins in with the audience to sing a song. Ours is an alternative rude adaptation of 'The Twelve Days of Christmas'. You might at this point be wondering how rude is rude. Well, see what you think!

Twelve boils a bursting,
Eleven painful swellings,
Ten crabs a-leaping,
Nine ulcers oozing,
Eight piles a-throbbing,
Seven blisters weeping,
Six scabs a-seeping,
Five cold sores,
Four haemorrhoids,
Three ripe zits,
Two pubic lice,
And a tape worm up my jacksey.

It won't make Broadway or even the local theatre, but everyone enjoys it and we usually raise about £500 for charity. The students get to see us making fools of ourselves so they absolutely love it.

(My thanks to Richard Cusden for giving me a copy of the song.)

ANGLING FOR A FIGHT

"Come on, quieten down." The door bangs open and the last of the students pile in. "Quickly now, find an empty place." Really this room, an A-level chemistry laboratory, is not the best one for these type of students, but the basic science lab wasn't available when the timetable was written. I hope to carry out a small practical with them after I've been through the theory. Their concentration level is very low so hands-on work keeps them focused.

It's a good job I had a very large dose of caffeine for lunch! I'm not keen on strong coffee, but if it helps me get through this lesson then I'll drink it. I start by calling out the register and note that they're all present. That's good as absences always provide me with stacks of paperwork. They must be keen, although I suspect for these Certificate of Pre-Vocational Education (CPVE) students, anything is better than school. I look up to find two students arguing.

"Stop that, you two! There's a lot of apparatus and chemical bottles in this lab." They're not a bad bunch; there are only a few who really try my patience. College, albeit for one day a week, seems to have a positive effect on their behaviour. I feel sorry for their schoolteachers. They must have a tough time. Some of these students are very tall and well built for their fifteen years. Most of them can barely write a sentence, so I give them a handout with blank spaces. All they have to do is fill out the correct missing words from the board. This way at least they have the theory written out for them.

"Right, now move the stools away to the side and we'll start the practical. Will you stop it, you two, or I'll throw you out and you know what will happen then. Back to school!"

They stop, but I can feel something is brewing between them. One of them is tall and a very nice, quiet lad. The other is much shorter and seems a pretty nasty piece of work. He appears to be goading the taller one.

"What is the problem?" I go over to the two of them, who now appear to be more than just arguing with each other. My goodness, the big lad has his hands around the other lad's throat! I try desperately to pull them apart, but they are more than a match for me. "Stop it at once! Let go!"

Oh good, a lecturer is walking through the lab. I shout at him but he is oblivious as to what is happening and walks straight out the door. The class are now egging him on. I'm still struggling to get them apart. I shout at one of the boys to go and get someone from the staff room. I'm still struggling, but at last manage to get them apart.

"Quiet!" I shout. A technician appears, obviously wondering what all the shouting is about. "Get the head of department quickly."

The class has now gone quiet. No amount of caffeine could have prepared me for this scenario! I turn to the two lads.

"What on Earth were you thinking of? You could be thrown off the course for this."

"Sorry," says the big lad.

The other one looks defiant and actually very smug. "I didn't start it, miss, he did."

The door finally opens and the head of department walks in. He dismisses the class and marches both boys away. I lock the lab and go to see the head. This has been brewing for a while. To be honest I would have felt like strangling the short one myself. They were both thrown off the course. I actually think they deserved it.

AN INCIDENT IN THE COMPUTER ROOM

"So, Mum, let's see if I've got this right. You were going to give it back to him?"

"Yes, I said so, didn't I?"

"And you didn't know if it was real or fake?"

"Yes, I just said so."

"I can't believe you did that."

"Well, I didn't really know. How could I? I've only ever seen one on television or in a newspaper."

"But didn't you think to ask someone and tell him you would give it back to him at the end of the day?"

"I never thought of that. I suppose I should have since most of my students come from an inner city, all very streetwise and certainly could have owned one. To be honest I wasn't thinking."

"No you can't have been. So tell me, how on Earth did it come to be in your possession anyway?"

"Well, as you know I don't like classrooms full of computers. I much prefer my chemistry laboratory with all the Bunsen burners, glassware and the periodic table. I can never understand why the assignments must be typed up – what's wrong with hand-written work like we produced in my day? Still, we must move with the times, I suppose, and at least they are more legible and easier to mark.

"I was sitting waiting for them to arrive when the door burst open and they all piled in laughing and chatting. That annoyed me to start with. They behave more like school kids than college students. I told them to take their seats quickly, only two per machine, to stop talking and to get their work out. I noticed that four of them were huddling together obviously looking at something. I went over and asked them what they had there that was so interesting. I took the small device from his hand and told him I was confiscating it until the end of the lesson and placed it in a desk drawer."

"Yes, yes, and then what happened?"

"They settled down and I must admit I did keep looking in the desk drawer. I kept wondering if it could be real. All of a sudden it was the end of the lesson and he was asking me if he could have it back. I took it out of the drawer and hesitated."

"I can't believe you were even thinking of giving it back to him."

"Well, I had never seen a real gun before, and, after all, it was his!"

"Please tell me you didn't?"

"No. I told him I was giving it to my head of department. He could deal with it."

JEALOUSY IN THE CLASSROOM

I really enjoy working here. I can't believe my luck. I worked in a laboratory for three years after finishing college but now I'm teaching, which is what I had wanted to do since being a little girl. I was lucky enough to get some part-time work here after I had my two children. Now I'm a full-time member of staff at this further education college teaching chemistry. It's a very large college in the centre of a large town, but unlike the surrounding colleges there are no green fields or gardens around it, just a few shrubs. It's a very old building, eleven storeys high, and each of the seven departments has their own floor.

I work in the science department. There are two large chemistry laboratories for the A-level students. The general studies department runs a one-year O-level revision course in various subjects and chemistry is one of them. This takes place in a small general science laboratory. Everyone calls this the coffin lab as the six benches are shaped like coffins. I can see all the students all of the time. It's brilliant.

I really like this class as it's made up of students of various ages and backgrounds. Most of them want to go on to do A-levels or some type of vocational training so they're all very keen. I have one who is a train driver but wants to go on to study engineering. It's a three-hour class, starting at 9.00, with a half-hour break in the middle. We do theory for the first half and practical for the second half. This is my last class of the week and I'm looking forward to 12.30.

I'm sitting in the break chatting to the laboratory technician who is setting out the apparatus for the practical. Then the door bursts open and all of the students pile in, all fifteen of them... Wait a minute, there were eighteen of them first thing this morning.

"Can one of you close the door and does anyone know where the other three students are?" I ask. Nobody says anything.

Suddenly the door flies open with a bang and a lecturer bursts through the door looking very red and flustered. I can't think what she wants; she's in the art and drama department, so we don't normally see her on this floor.

She starts shouting at the top of her voice, "You've got to come downstairs immediately. There are three of your students outside causing a rumpus."

"My students! I didn't give birth to them, you know. They're just in my class."

I pop my head into the prep room. "Can you keep an eye on the class for me while I go downstairs?"

"Yes, of course," someone replies.

"Okay, lead the way," I say to the lecturer.

I rush down the stairs close behind her and out of the building. Oh my goodness, there are lots of students standing around cheering, jeering and shouting! What is happening? In the middle of the crowd I spot my three missing students. The girl is standing looking a little lonely among the crowd and crying. There's a fight going on between the two boys. One of the crowd turns to me and says that there is a lot of jealousy between the two boys over this particular girl.

"Do something!" the art and drama lecturer says.

"What exactly do you want me to do?

"Take it off him!"

"You're kidding." I turn to her. "Get security, quick. I can't do anything. I'm not trained in the martial arts and I'm certainly not going to try to wrestle a large machete from the boy who is trying to kill the other one with it!"

AGAINST THE RULES

"I want you to know I am really glad you asked me to come on this trip with you and your students. As a secretary, I don't usually get asked. Hey, are you listening to me? You're miles away. Penny for them?"

"I'm thinking unemployed, no money."

"Stop it right now. They will be here. It's just that small group of students – all the others are here."

"Yes, I know. But you always get a few who think they can get away with anything without consequences."

"But who does this group include, eh?"

"Well, yes, but you had his written approval and the rules apply to all of them, including her. It doesn't matter that she is his daughter."

"But he's my head of department!"

"Irrelevant."

"Well, to you maybe, but he's not your boss." I hear the loud noise of the train doors locking. I look at my watch; it's five minutes before the train leaves.

"Now don't panic. I'm sure if you ask the official nicely in your best German, plead if you have to, they will make an exception in this case."

"I don't think so. German trains are always punctual and Germans definitely do not approve of breaking the rules. When they say the doors are locked five minutes before departure and no-one else can get on, they mean it."

"Look, there they are."

I tap my watch, but from their faces they're beginning to panic. I did warn them. Here goes. I walk up to the guard and smile at him.

"Excuse me, sir, there is a group of my students on the platform, and I know it's against the rules, but could you possibly let them on?" I hope my German is correct. There is a pause that seems like an eternity, but then there is a loud noise and the doors open.

Four very relieved students dive on the train. "Now let that be a lesson to you, sit down and be quiet. You're lucky I speak German," I say.

I remind them of the college rules: "If any of you miss a bus or train due to lateness the group will not wait for you, and you will have to make your own way back to the guesthouse at your own expense."

Would I have really left them? Thankfully, I'll never know.

THE TENNIS RACKET

I examine the tennis racket. It couldn't be, could it? It's very slightly misshapen. I love charity shops. I often look around them in my lunch hour. As you rummage through the items you wonder about all the people who have donated their unwanted belongings. Some of them look quite new, not wanted anymore, so many reasons they are here in the basket or on the shelves.

The racket is definitely not new as it's a bit old-fashioned, but it's still serviceable. It could be given to a child to practise with or simply to use in the garden. A thought just jumped into my mind. I have seen it very recently. My thoughts are interrupted.

"Excuse me, are you interested in that racket, madam? A lad bought it in a few hours ago. He said he didn't need it any more," says the shop assistant.

"Really? What did he look like?" I ask.

"I didn't take much notice. Medium height, weight, dark hair. I asked him why he was donating it. 'If you don't you want it I could always take it to another shop,' he said. 'Oh, no, lovely we'll have it, thank you,' I told him. Then he hurried out. Very strange if you ask me," she said.

I think to myself, it couldn't be, could it? Remorse perhaps? Not him. I think back to the day of the incident. I had been summoned out of class yet again. One of my students had been seen in the foyer and I had to come down at once. I knew immediately who it was. He should have been in my lesson. What is it this time? I thought as I rushed down the stairs and through the double doors. There was an argument in progress between my student and another student, who I didn't know, and the caretaker. He had a tennis racket in his hand and the other one was clutching his head and shouting. The caretaker seemed to be trying to calm the situation. Other students were egging them on.

"Give me that racket. Now," I demanded. I was shaking, although I'm not sure whether it was with anger or fright. "What has happened here?" I asked the injured boy.

"He hit me over the head with the racket, miss."

I shouted at my student again. He turned to face me and the caretaker grabbed the racket.

"What on Earth possessed you?" I asked.

"He tried to grab it from me, miss, and I retaliated," my student said.

"What, by hitting him on the head with it? Very civilised!" I turned to the poor lad who was still clutching his head. "Did you try to grab it?"

"Well, he was waving it about and I thought he would hit someone with it."

I was so tempted to say to him, 'Well, yes he did, you unfortunately,' but I didn't. "Are you in pain? Do you want me to call someone?"

"No, I'm okay. Can we just leave it? I probably shouldn't have tried to grab it."

"If you're sure."

I took the racket from my student and handed it to the caretaker and told him to get to my class. "The head of department will deal with you later."

I've always wondered what happened afterwards. I wasn't even called in to see the head about the incident. Well, he obviously got his racket back. Perhaps he felt remorse after all. I looked at it again.

"No, thanks. I'll leave it," I tell the shop assistant. As I leave the shop I think that perhaps the best place for it would be the dustbin.

THE CONCENTRATED ACID INCIDENT

"I can see an anxious time ahead for some of you," I say, as one student shudders. "Don't worry, I'll make sure that this experiment is completed without a hitch." Famous last words.

"But, miss, concentrated hydrochloric acid is highly corrosive and dangerous, isn't it?"

"Yes, but we're going to follow the health and safety rules for its use. You're all wearing lab coats. Make sure all the buttons are done up and that it fits you properly. Safety glasses on – not cool, I know, but better than losing your eyesight. You two who wear glasses, here are goggles to put over the top of them. Make sure there are no holes in your plastic gloves, and let me have a look at your shoes. I'm pleased to see no sandals today. You all look like real chemists."

"But, miss, it still sounds dangerous. It can form an acid mist, can't it?"

"Look, let's get this in proportion, shall we? Have any of you been in an ironmonger's shop, or looked in your dad's shed or the garage, or under the sink at the cleaning materials in your kitchen, come to that? It's sold as 'spirits of salts' and can be used to unblock sinks and descale enamel. All of these precautions are on the bottle. You wouldn't be worried about using it at home, would you? Right, I have been through the instructions, including the use of the separating

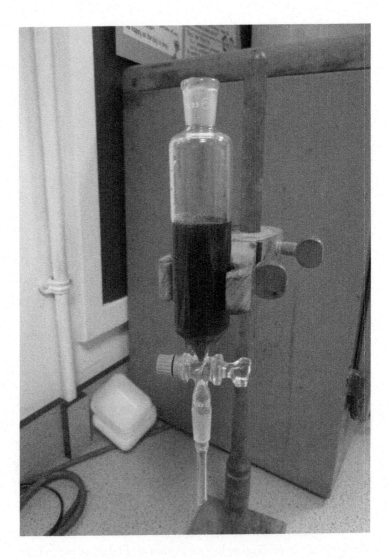

funnel, so collect all your apparatus and away you go." I walk around the laboratory and everything seems to be fine.

All of a sudden I hear a shout. "Miss, miss! Help! My separating funnel is leaking. Take it!"

She thrusts it into my hand and the contents splatter all over my legs. I look down at once to see my tights disintegrating. I can feel the acid burning my legs. Can't they follow simple instructions, for goodness sake? Obviously not…

I need to get to some running water immediately. I call out for the technician, trying not to sound panicky, and place the funnel in the sink. "Keep an eye on the class for me, will you? Before the acid starts to corrode my skin."

I rush to the toilet and splash my legs with copious amounts of water. Why didn't she follow my instructions, which are underlined? If there's a problem, put the funnel into the sink where you're working. It said absolutely nothing about handing it to your teacher!

THE SQUARE HOLE

"It's lovely to sit down and take the weight off your feet, isn't it? Relax…well, almost relax. These airports are so clean, light and airy, aren't they? I also get to practise my German. I think I'll buy a newspaper. That will keep me occupied for weeks and I can use it as a teaching tool in my beginners German class. I wonder where the students are. Have you seen them?"

"Yes, look, they're over there. What a week. They've certainly kept us on our toes. I don't know about you but I'm shattered. I'll need at least a week to recover."

"You're not kidding. Overall, though, they weren't bad – certainly better than last year. Only a couple of hiccups, but nothing we couldn't handle. Mind you I kept an eye on them in the duty free. Trouble is many of them appear over eighteen."

"Of course, they could have made their purchases in the local supermarket. Remember, you commented on one particular student who had a basket full of German meat, savouries and sweets and that really large bottle of wine, which he assured me was for his mum? He could hardly lift his case."

"I thought that was a bit odd as I knew they weren't allowed to drink. Shh, he's coming over. Good grief! Whatever you do don't laugh."

"I'll try not to but you have to admit it's quite funny."

"Miss, look what someone's done to my case!"

I stifle a laugh, as does my colleague, and try to appear concerned.

"What happened to your case?"

"They asked me what I was carrying and they wanted to see inside. I couldn't find the keys. I searched everywhere. I told them what I had bought for the family. I think they didn't believe me and then they did this. Mum will be furious! She had to buy this case for me to come on the trip, and now look at the side of it! What am I going to say to her? I don't think I can even claim on the insurance."

"It's a very neat job but it is a very large hole. About nine inches at a guess. Let's hope your mum sees the funny side of it and enjoys all the food and drink you've bought for her!"

THE SCIENCE DEPARTMENT VERSION OF BLIND DATE

I can hear the music and I'm feeling very nervous. We haven't had a lot of practice. Fortunately, I don't actually have many speaking lines. I adjust my red wig and make sure my short skirt is straight and not showing too much leg.

I soon hear: "It's *Blind Date*. Please welcome Miss Cilla Black."

I take a deep breath and enter the room. I stand frozen to the spot, looking around me. All I can see are hundreds of faces on the tiered seating, staring at me. I wonder how many of my students are in the audience. These high-heeled shoes are killing me. The sun is streaming through the large windows onto the screen in front of the white-boards. The three contestants are sitting behind the screen hidden from my view. I walk around to them and they are sitting on wooden stools. What a sight! Three male lecturers dressed as women. The best description of them is a washerwoman, a tart and a nerd. I smile.

"I know you all come from Kingston but what are your names and what do you do in your spare time? Number one?" I ask.

"I really enjoy having fun with my best friend."

"Number two?"

"I enjoy drinking at our local social club with friends."

"Number three?"

"I'm writing a book on the history of the town."

Their answers bring howls of laughter and wolf whistles. I walk back to my place.

"Now let me introduce the contestant who will pick one of these lovely ladies for a date." In walks the man looking for a love match. He is tall, well built and quite good-looking. "Hello and welcome. Tell us your name and where you're from."

"I'm Matti and I live in Kingston."

"What do you do for a living, Matti?"

"I'm a maths lecturer."

"What do you do in your spare time?"

"I love walking and visiting old houses."

"That must be very interesting."

Boos come from some of the audience.

"So, let's hear your first question," I say.

"Teaching is a very demanding profession, so I like to go to bed very early. How would you feel about that, number one?"

"That would be absolutely fine by me but you wouldn't get a lot of sleep."

"Number three?"

"I need my beauty sleep so no problem there."

"Number two?"

"As long as you shower first and have clean night attire."

I pause till the laughter subsides. "And your second question?"

"I like watching films and plays on television. What kinds of programme interest you, number two?"

"I prefer soaps. My favourite is EastEnders." The audience seems divided on this answer. The girls cheer and the boys boo.

"Number one?"

"Historical plays, such as *Jack the Ripper*, are just up my street, so to speak." Again howls of laughter.

"Number three?"

"Documentaries which broaden my mind. I often take notes while I'm watching them."

The students groan.

"And your last question?"

"I like taking holidays abroad in the sun. Do you enjoy them as well, number one?"

"I most certainly do. The people are much more laid back."

"Number three?"

"As long as there are plenty of castles and churches to visit." More groans from the audience.

"Number two?"

"The beach must be clean and I love the water."

I say, "Now, Matti, it's nearly make-your-mind-up time. But before you do, our Graham will give you a quick reminder."

"Contestant number one can really show you a good time. Contestant number two loves water and clean living. Contestant number three would love to educate you. The choice is yours," said our Graham.

The students start to chant and clap. "One, one, one, one, one!"

"I choose number one." More clapping.

Number two and number three come out and Matti hugs them and says goodbye with relief.

"Are you ready? Matti your blind date for tonight is contestant number one." She comes around the screen in an extremely tight fitting dress ready for a hug. All of a sudden I find myself being picked up and flung over Matti's shoulder.

"What are you doing? This wasn't in the script!" The students are standing up and chanting. There are lots of wolf whistles. More, more!

"I don't fancy any of them. I'll take you instead."

"Help, help!" As he walks out of the room I only hope my skirt is long enough to cover my bottom!

CHEMISTRY IS FUN FOR PARENTS TOO

"Hey, Dad, I'm really getting excited. I haven't been in a proper chemistry lab before."

"Nor have I, Son."

"But, Dad, you work here. You're always moaning about the students."

"Yes, but not in the science department. I must admit I'm quite looking forward to seeing what they get up to in their laboratories. Remember my office is on a different floor in general studies."

"But you must meet other deputy heads. You're always having meetings."

"We hold those on the first floor in one of the conference rooms."

"How boring."

"Right, we're here."

"Can we go up in the lift?"

"No, don't be so lazy. The stairs will keep you fit."

"Oh, all right. Race you!"

"We want the third floor. They call it the coffin lab, I believe."

"Wow, do they have real coffins in it? Wait till I tell them at school. I did science in a lab with coffins in."

"No, silly, the benches are shaped like coffins."

"Oh, that's a shame. We're here, Dad. I think we're last. I'll open the door. There are lots of people in here and it smells funny."

"Well, it is a chemistry lab."

"Hello, Mrs C. This looks interesting."

"Hi, Steve. First time up here, I believe?"

"Dad's scared of the coffin lab."

"Shush, you."

"Nice to see you. I hope you and your son enjoy the evening."

"You bet, eh, Dad? Let's work here. Cool! We get to wear lab coats and safety glasses. Look at all the chemicals and glassware. And a Bunsen burner."

"How do you know what that is?"

"Oh, I forgot to tell you. I went to visit my new school with Mum a while ago and the chemistry teacher gave us a short guided tour and there were some kids using them in a lab. She told me I would be using one."

"Right, welcome, everyone, to this 'Chemistry is fun for parents too' evening," I start.

"She looks nice, Dad. Who's she?"

"She's one of the chemists."

"I hope my science teacher at my new school looks like her, with long blond hair. Why is she wearing big thick rubber gloves? And what's in the container? There's vapour pouring out of it."

"Weren't you listening? It's liquid nitrogen. It's so cold it will freeze a person's fingers off."

"Oh, look, the petals have fallen off the flower she put in the container and she's just smashed a banana to pieces on the bench. So what do they use it for then?"

"Er, you'll learn about that when you're older."

"Dad, you're blushing. I'm nearly ten you know. Look, what's the man doing with those balloons?"

"Listen to Mrs C!"

"Here we have a hydrogen balloon and because it's lighter than air Brian is going to put it on the ceiling and set light to it. I hope the mix is right, Brian, otherwise we might set fire to the ceiling! Prepare for the bang, everyone."

"Look at that flame shooting out, and flipping hell that bang made me jump!"

"Dad, Dad, can she do it again? That was awesome."

"Of course we can young man. Ready, steady, go."

"Blimey, there's a big black mark on the ceiling."

"Now, children, it's your turn to do some practical."

"This is ace, Dad."

"Shush and listen to her instructions."

"Do you know the teacher on our bench, Dad?"

"No, but I recognise him from some of our meetings. He is a biologist, I think."

"Make sure you all have plastic gloves on and safety glasses. That includes parents, Steve. The instructions are on your bench and the teacher will guide you. Just remember that concentrated hydrochloric acid is corrosive, so be very careful with it."

"Did you hear that, Dad? It's dangerous. Wicked! I've put a few crystals of the potassium chloride on this watch glass. Now for the acid."

"Only a few drops, she said."

"All right, I was listening. Stop nagging. Now I dip the nichrome wire in the mixture and place it in the Bunsen flame. Look at the colour of the flame! This lilac is my sister's favourite colour. According to this chart there are potassium ions present. John is going to be so jealous. I can't wait to tell him. Let's do the others. That's it, I've done them all, so what's next?"

"Your last experiment is making nylon."

"Cor! We can do this as well! I *know*, I must listen carefully to her instructions. Don't fuss, Dad. She knows what she's doing."

"You have two small beakers on your bench labelled 'A' for aqueous diamine solution and 'B' for decanedioyl dichloride in cyclohexane. You're going to carefully pour the contents of beaker B into beaker A, but – this is the important bit – you pour it very slowly and carefully down the glass rod that's on your bench. This solution will float on top of the solution in beaker A. If you look carefully at the interface of the two solutions you'll see a greyish film of nylon. Then, using the tweezers, you'll pick up a little of this and lift it slowly from the beaker. You can wind this onto the other glass rod on your bench. The teacher on your bench will help you."

"Gosh, this is ace. Right, here I go. Wow, it's working! Look, look, I'm making nylon."

"Are you okay, Son? You seem to be coughing. In fact, my throat is tickling now and other people in the room are also coughing."

"Dad, Mrs C is telling us to leave the lab as we're going to have some refreshments. I want to carry on! This is fantastic. I don't want to stop. The teachers are putting all the beakers in a large glass-fronted cupboard in the corner and it's making a really loud noise."

"Come on, Son, or you'll miss the orange juice and your favourite biscuits."

"Oh, I was having so much fun." Dad pushes him out in the corridor and towards the stairs to the canteen.

"After your eats you're going to have your photograph taken. I'm hoping that we will get a mention in the newspaper."

"I can't wait for school tomorrow to tell all my mates. They'll be gobsmacked.

"Why did the evening finish so suddenly?"

"Well, apparently we were inhaling a small amount of hydrogen chloride fumes, which are formed during the experiment, which made everyone cough. One of the solutions was inadvertently made up too weak so it wasn't able to mop up all the hydrogen chloride produced by the reaction. This gas can irritate the lungs. But we were in capable hands and there was certainly no danger. I think everyone really enjoyed it and I'm quite sure that all of you were inspired by the event."

"You're not kidding! What a story to tell my friends."

A MYSTERY

I hate these dark, dank, misty mornings. I leave very early every day, because the traffic on the main road gets really heavy after 7.30. I use a minor road for the first part of my journey, only joining the motorway for the second half of it. This journey is much worse in the winter months, and today, as it's nearly Christmas, it's even worse.

On top of that, I'm earlier than usual this particular morning, as I have to set up an experiment for the first lesson. As there's no car park in the school grounds, I have to park my car in a side road; fortunately, it's only a short walk to the school. I check I've locked the car and hurry towards the school gate. As I enter, I'm sure I can hear footsteps behind me. I look around but can't see anyone. It's just someone else going into work early as well, I expect, but I still quicken my pace. At last I'm in the building, and quickly wend my way up to the staffroom to make myself a tea. With a cup in hand, I make my way to my classroom.

It's quite dark in the school, with just the emergency lights to guide me. It's quite a long walk to my classroom. It's at the far end of the building at the end of a long corridor. Normally I like it, as it's away from all the noise and disruptions of the pupils. As I unlock the door and switch on the light I hear that noise again. No, it couldn't be... Nobody else would be down here this early in the morning.

A shiver runs down my spine. Pull yourself together, I tell myself. It's only a school, for goodness' sake – although admittedly a very large one, in which pupils can disappear along one corridor before you can make it up the first flight of stairs. It's like a rabbit warren. And, of course, at this time of year and in the morning there is no daylight at all.

Now, where is that list of equipment I need for the science demonstration? There it is. I pick up the tray and go into the preparation room next door. Carefully, I place beakers, conical flasks, pipettes, and the solutions I will need on it. There's that noise again. I put the tray down and look out the door. Still nobody there! I must be hearing things.

I look up at the clock and it's nearly eight. Good, the staff should be coming in soon, and anyway, where is the technician? He's usually here by now. I pick up the tray to take it back to my classroom when the door behind me flies open.

The glassware that I had so carefully arranged on my tray is now rolling about and I just stop myself from dropping it. I can hear my heart beating loudly.

"Miss, miss, didn't you hear me? I've been trying to catch you. I saw you get out of your car. You've left your lights on!"

THE BUNSEN BURNER

Goodness me, I'm bored! His voice is droning on and on. I look out of the window and sigh. The sun is shining and I'm stuck in here listening to this man wittering on. Just how long does it take for our head of science to show us the correct way to light a Bunsen burner safely? He has been talking now for ten minutes and I have to say I haven't really been listening. After all, three of us are qualified science teachers and I'm quite sure that the trainee teachers have used a Bunsen before. I wonder if we should be taking notes. This must be the most boring of our training sessions so far. Still, I suppose health and safety is very important when teaching science, especially where chemistry is concerned.

"Have you got that? Any questions?" His voice brings me back to the meeting. "No? Right, we will have a practice."

We all file into the laboratory next door and follow his instructions to the letter. Suddenly, there are eight Bunsen burners springing into life and burning brightly with yellow flames.

"Well done," he says. How patronising. We turn off the taps and head out of the door in silence. Goodness, it's been a long day.

A couple of weeks later I'm standing in front of a class of thirty fresh-faced twelve-year-olds. The topic, you guessed it, is lighting

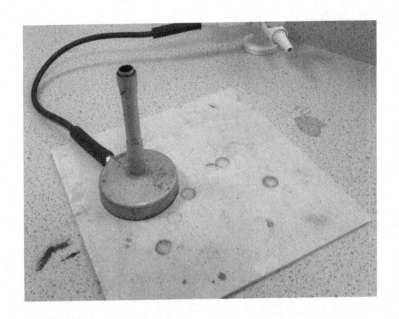

a Bunsen burner. I'm absolutely confident I know exactly what to do. What could go wrong? In this laboratory there are four long wooden benches, each with four double gas taps and two sinks.

"Spread out now so there's one pair with one Bunsen to a double tap." I feel they would be too squashed for two pairs to share the taps, and I can observe them more easily if they are well spread out. I've already placed one set of apparatus at each double tap.

"Class, follow the instructions that I've written on the board," I say.

Just to make sure, I go through the steps one at a time. "Put one end of the rubber tubing on one of the taps on the bench in front of you and the other on the Bunsen. Make sure that the tubing is firmly on both the tap and Bunsen. Turn the hole to the closed position and place the Bunsen on the heat-proof mat. Put your safety glasses on and button up your lab coats. Stop talking at the back and listen! This is important. Make sure your hair is tied back. Yes, even you, boys."

I walk around the class checking each one carefully. I'm leaving nothing to chance. They're all set up perfectly and I haven't forgotten anything. I feel quite smug! What was all the fuss about at that training session?

"So, using your splint, one of you take a light from the lit Bunsen in the middle of your bench, turn on the gas tap and light your Bunsen burner."

They soon spring into life and I can see all the yellow flames. Suddenly there is an almighty bang and a massive yellow flame shoots across one of the benches. The kids let out a massive scream. What on Earth is happening? I rush and switch off the tap. Would you believe it? One pupil has attached the Bunsen to one tap and opened the other tap by mistake!

Well, you know what they say about the best-laid plans of mice and men. Nothing could have prepared me for that, not even our head of science!

THE PHOTO

I wake up to a lovely sunny day and hope that it's a good omen. I think very carefully about what I'm going to wear on my first day at a new school. As I brush my teeth I look up at the photo frame on my bathroom shelf and chuckle to myself. As I drive towards the school I wonder how I will get on. My impression of it at my interview hadn't been too bad, although it will be tough, as any school in special measures always is. I hope I can make a difference.

I go into the classroom, prepare for the lesson and wait for the bell to ring.

Here they come! Suddenly I'm faced with thirty kids of a year ten class. This first contact could make or break my authority in the classroom for the rest of the year. They're staring at me, summing me up and waiting. "I'm…" My mind flashes back to the photo frame sitting proudly on my bathroom shelf. It's a newspaper cutting with a photo about saucy thieves running off with village signs. The nameplates at either end of the main street of this particular village have been stolen five times. I had read the article and how I had laughed. But now it doesn't seem so funny. What possessed me to marry a man with such a surname? I needn't have changed my name to his. Many women nowadays don't, but he is very proud of it, and he would have been very hurt. In fact, I know a very successful head teacher with the same surname.

"I'm..." I falter and change tack. "Okay. Do you know anything about cricket?"

"Yes, miss," the boys reply eagerly.

"Well, my husband's cousin is a very famous cricketer who is actually now an England umpire."

"Who is he, miss?"

"Peter Willey."

"So your name is Mrs Willey then?"

"Yes, that's right," and I write it in large letters on the board. No muffled laughs or titters. That went well, I think.

My mind goes back to the photo frame in my bathroom. A man is carrying a sign saying 'Willey, please drive carefully'. The headline reads: 'Keep your hands off our Willey.'

Only six more classes to go! It could be a very long day.

KEEP YOUR HANDS OFF OUR WILLEY

Ready for erection . . . new sign arrives in the village   Picture: PETER LEA

THE INSPECTION

I've been lying here awake for what seems like an eternity. I look over at the clock. It's only 2.00. What is the matter with me? They're only school kids. Who am I kidding? They're year nines and they are dreadful. Thirteen is a difficult age as they're now teenagers going through puberty. At least when they get to year ten they're starting their GCSEs so their behaviour normally improves. Unfortunately, in this particular school it takes a little longer. Mind you, not all of them are very difficult, but this one particular class is the worst.

Tomorrow will be a nightmare. Even the word sends shivers down my spine. The school inspector. It's not as if I'm new to teaching. I've been through lots of inspections over the years, but this one will be torment. Oh, we've had meetings to discuss tactics for coping with unruly pupils, but we're on the front line. Thank goodness the powers that be have decided to have two of us in the classroom for this particular group!

But what I need at this moment is to go back to sleep. I look over at my husband. He's sleeping like a baby without a care in the world. I mustn't wake him. When I mentioned it yesterday he was very supportive. Mind you he doesn't really understand as he only deals with adults in his job. I lie back down and close my eyes.

*

Suddenly I hear a bell ringing and sit up with a start. I switch off the alarm and jump out of bed. Take your time, I say to myself, and keep calm. What am I talking about keep calm? I go downstairs and make myself a very strong mug of coffee. I force myself to eat some toast, jump in the car and head towards school.

It's a very large school of about 1500 pupils. Too large, really. Too many stairs and corridors. As I enter the classroom I see the inspector is already there and talking with my female colleague. The inspector is a woman. Personally, I would have preferred a man, as I have usually found female inspectors to be unsympathetic to women teachers. I don't know why. She seems pleasant enough, but that could be a façade. Trouble is I couldn't flutter my eyelashes at a woman!

I can hear all the pupils outside the door making a racket. The bell goes and they all pile in, but without pushing and shoving for a change. Obviously they've had a stern chat from their tutor. They sit down and get their pens and workbooks out and I hand around the textbooks. So far so good. We start the lesson and for once the pupils seem quite attentive, and a couple of them even ask fairly sensible questions. At this point I'm wondering if an alien class has replaced our usual one!

After half an hour the inspector indicates that she has seen enough and is leaving. As she goes out of the door she says: "Well done. There will be a debriefing in the break."

"Thank you." I close the door behind her.

There is a short pause before all hell breaks loose in the classroom. We duck as a couple of books fly past our heads hitting two lads on the other side of the room. Two others fight over a calculator. Two of the girls climb up onto their desks and jump across the front ones, then disappear out of the door. It's absolute mayhem. The two of us sit back and wait for the bell while the remaining pupils seem to calm down. My colleague looks at me.

"What do you think?" she asks.

"Well, let's give them their due. At least they behaved them-selves for the inspector, which was a miracle in itself. I think she was quite impressed and we should get a good report."

Although the bell hasn't gone we thank the remaining pupils and chorus together: "Class dismissed."

They crash out the door and disappear into the warren of corridors before we change our minds. Suddenly the door opens and in walks the deputy head. "Quick," I whisper, "what's our excuse for letting them out early?"

"Ladies, I've just come to congratulate you. The inspector has given you a grade one for this class. I'll see you for a chat in my office when you're ready." He closes the door behind him.

"Well, that's a turn-up for the book. I'll never run down a woman inspector again."

COTTON WOOL AND FIRE DON'T MIX

From out of nowhere I become aware of thick, grey, billowing clouds of smoke. I choke and, as I see flames leaping into the air, my heart starts to pound. It gets hotter and hotter. I'm sweating profusely. I have to get out of here, I think, but my legs feel like lead and won't move. I can't run; I seem to be glued to the floor.

Suddenly there's a loud ringing that sounds like a fire alarm. I'm panic-stricken. I'm going to die. Where is everyone? I feel someone shaking me and I open my eyes and see my husband at the side of the bed looking rather worried. Then I see the alarm clock flashing.

"Are you okay?" he asks.

"I am now." I was obviously having a nightmare. It was so real. I had better get up. I feel very hot and sticky. I must have a shower before I eat breakfast.

"I'll make you a nice strong cup of tea."

"Thanks."

Eating my toast, I can't stop thinking about the dream. It had seemed so real. I gather up my books and briefcase for work, reach for my car keys and am soon on my way.

I like Wednesdays as I have an hour before my first class and always use it for preparing lessons. Today is no different. I sit down to mark but find my mind wandering as usual. I can see a student

setting up an experiment. He must be a second-year chemistry student carrying out a project, as I can't see his teacher anywhere. I don't know why but I'm interested to see what he's doing. It doesn't take much to distract me. I peek and see he's set up a conical flask with granules of a metal and a clear liquid, probably an acid. It's sitting on a tripod and gauze over a Bunsen burner. Not a problem, I think, as he has a pair of safety glasses on.

I go into the laboratory and cast my eyes quickly over his apparatus to check it's safe.

"Are you okay? Do you need any help?"

"No, thank you." He appears very confident about the experiment. "I'm measuring the rate of gas produced from hydrochloric acid and various metals. If I need anything I'll come and ask you."

I go back to my marking but I can't concentrate. My mind drifts back to my nightmare. It had been so vivid. Suddenly I look up and see him wrapping a large wad of cotton wool around the flask. What is he going to do? He's holding a lighted splint and, oh my goodness he's going to light the Bunsen with it.

My nightmare flashes before me. "Stop, stop!" I yell,, running towards him. I stretch out my hand and grab the lighted splint. "What are you doing?" He looks startled, totally unaware of the potential danger.

"I need to regulate the heat, miss, and cotton wool seemed like a good insulator." I stared at him. Could he really not see the danger? Obviously not! By now he seemed a bit agitated. "No harm done. Let's sort you out with the proper apparatus. Okay, I'll just be next door. Shout if you need me."

I sit down. If I hadn't had that dream, I think to myself, I might not have taken any notice of him. Fire and hydrogen definitely form a lethal combination. An explosion and fire, no less!

THE URINE SAMPLE

I look around the room, feeling pleased with my work. Everything is ready for the class. I glance at the clock. There are only a couple of minutes to go. Then the bell rings and they all pile in, laughing and chattering.

"'Ere, miss, what's with the new arrangement of the tables?"

"I thought this would be better. It means you will all be able to see me and I'll be able to see all of you. No hiding at the back. I'm sure you will learn a lot more." They all groan. "Sit down and get your books out." This horseshoe arrangement of tables will make it easier to keep this class in order. At sixteen and repeating GCSE, these students don't have the best attitude to learning.

"What we doing today, miss?"

"Well, last week you learnt all about the functions of the kidney, so today you're going to carry out a practical on the liquid by-product secreted by the kidneys, which is...?"

"Urine, miss."

"Lovely, I don't think."

"What was that, Jack?"

"Nothing, miss, but I bet it isn't really urine."

"What makes you say that? In previous lessons you've handled real lungs, livers and kidneys. So why wouldn't we have real urine?

Get into pairs and put a lab coat on. Tie your hair back too. We don't want it contaminating the samples. Stand by one of the sets of apparatus and the four small beakers of urine. You have two reagents in dropper bottles. They are blue biuret solution and blue Benedict's solution. The labels you see have fallen off samples from patients in the laboratory of a hospital." The labels are:

1   A pregnant patient with swollen ankles – sample is high in protein, but normal in colour and has no sugar.
2   A boy with a broken arm – sample has no protein or sugar and is normal in colour.
3   A farmer working in the fields on a hot day, who fell and cut his hand – sample has no sugar or protein, but is dark in colour due to dehydration.
4   A girl feeling very unwell with blurred vision – sample is normal in colour, no protein but sugar present.

"You're going to test the samples and link them with the description of each patient. You will test for sugar and protein and observe the colour intensity of each sample. Here is a handout to fill in for your findings. Right, you have thirty minutes."

The Bunsen burners burst into flame and they start busying themselves with the task. They love practicals and it's a great sight to see. I wander around.

"That's a lovely deep purple colour from the biuret, so what's present?"

"Protein, miss."

"Yes that's correct. What about the colour of the sample?"

"It's normal pale yellow. But, miss, there's no red solid when I heat it with Benedict's solution so we reckon there's no sugar in this sample."

"So which patient is it then?"

"The pregnant lady."

"Excellent. Now repeat with the other three samples." I move around the other students.

When they are all finished they sit back in their seats. "Let's see how you got on." All the pairs seem to have the correct answers. I'm really pleased with them. "Just one more thing before you go. Can you remember from last week what a person may be suffering from if they have sugar in their urine? Yes, Sam."

"Diabetes, miss."

"Excellent. And what would you notice about it?"

"It can have a sweet odour"

"Yes, but not just an odour. Years ago, when people had a family doctor, they would use a very quick and simple test before sending a sample to the hospital."

"What's that, miss?"

"After smelling it, the doctor would dip his finger in the sample just like I'm doing now and then taste it like this." I put my finger in my mouth. "Hmm, very sweet." Their faces are a picture! Am I joking or not?

THE DUSTBIN LID

This little extra teaching job hasn't been as bad as I thought. In fact, to tell the truth, I was dreading it. I don't know what possessed me to agree to it in the first place. But the head seemed really nice and said I would be really helping her out. One of the staff had left at short notice and the GCSEs were coming up. I mean, I didn't need the money as I was earning enough already even though I wasn't full time. Did I need the experience? No. Not this kind!

Anyway, here I am waiting for the class of four sixteen-year-olds to appear. Here they are now with a teaching assistant. She will stay for the whole lesson and lend a hand if I need it. To be honest these kids seem okay, although perhaps that's because there are two of us.

"What we doing today, miss?"

"Are you going to do an experiment, miss?"

"Will there be explosions, miss?"

"Will it be dangerous, miss?"

"Slow down. Get your paper and pens out ready to take a few notes. You're going to learn about change of state. I'm placing these orange crystals in this boiling tube. You can see they are just covering the bottom of the tube. I'm going to heat the tube in a Bunsen burner and I want you to write down what you see happening."

I light the Bunsen burner and place the boiling tube in the flame.

"Wow. It's changing into green tea leaves!"

"Look at them shooting out of the tube! You be careful, miss."

"This is brilliant, miss!"

"We've never seen anything like this before."

They are very well behaved and write everything down. So much so, I wonder why they need to be here. I can hear a rumpus next door but I had often heard the same thing at my last place, so I simply ignore it. I do, however, wonder why these four lads are in this school in the first place. When I finish, the assistant leads them out to collect their coats.

I pick up my belongings and make my way to my car. As I open the car door a blanket of heat hits me. Wow, it's hot in here. One of those dog days. As I sit down in front of the steering wheel I realise I'm hemmed in. I do wish people would park their cars sensibly. I had thought I would be okay here but some idiot has blocked me in. I'll have to wait about five minutes but at least I have a bit of shade by this hedge. I listen to the very loud voices of the mums. If they always shout at their kids like this then I can see why their children have been sent here for bad behaviour!

My thoughts are unexpectedly interrupted as the exit door smashes open and one of the lads I have just been teaching strolls out. Now, he isn't doing anything particularly bad, just behaving like a typical sixteen-year-old coming out of school. His mother, however, starts loudly screeching at him. Fleetingly, I feel sorry for him with a mother like that.

Without warning, he picks up a dustbin lid from a bin outside the door and throws it at her. Quite frankly, I don't blame him. She grabs him by the ear and, still shouting obscenities at him, drags him to her car. I'm sorely tempted to get out of my car and go over to give her a piece of my mind, but I don't. She would probably attack me. I bet he'll get a good hiding when he gets home. Totally unjustified! Now I know why I turned down the headmistress' offer of a job earlier today.

Well, working for a school for difficult teenagers wasn't quite what I had in mind when I took up teaching.

THE MOBILE PHONE INCIDENT

I do love my cup of tea in the morning. None of your decaffeinated stuff. I like it strong, sweet and with its four per cent caffeine. I know this amount as one of my experiments is the extraction of caffeine from ordinary tea. A drug it may be, but legal it is, and I need to be alert today. I have four classes of retake GCSE science groups one after the other. Over-sixteen students full of hormones who are forced, in a way, to study a subject they either hated or found difficult at school. Whoever drew up my timetable had obviously never taught these classes.

As I sip my second cup, my thoughts wander to some of the students. One in particular springs to mind. I interviewed him at length on induction day and he seemed a nice enough lad, though not really suited to further education in my humble opinion. I asked him why he doesn't just get a job. He sat there looking at me as if butter wouldn't melt in his mouth. I had heard it all before. You know full well they were probably troublemakers at school but of course their references can't say that. He assured me he was keen, which wasn't a word I would have used for him, and would work hard to pass the exam. Apparently, he didn't fancy a dead-end job. The trouble is they all say that. I'm sure most of them say what they think we want to hear. What they really mean is that they don't really want to work but instead they want to while away a year doing nothing at college. I listened carefully to his answers for about ten minutes and made a note in my diary, but in the end I said we would give him a chance. I should have known. I had been teaching these type of lads long enough!

I arrive early to work and make myself a final cup of tea before the onslaught. The seating in this particular laboratory is definitely not conducive to teaching these type of students. They need to be seated in such a way that I can see all of them all of the time. I prefer loose tables that I can move around according to the size of the class. However, this room is old-fashioned and has static benches either side of an aisle.

The bell rings. Here we go. They pile in and I ask them all to at least sit on one side of the aisle. The back row is appealing to those who don't want to be here. I call the register and am pleased they're all present.

I start to talk. I look up and see the student from my breakfast thoughts this morning clearly not listening to me. Well, he's certainly not taking notes. I call out to him to put his mobile phone away.

He looks me straight in the eye. "I'm not using my phone, miss."

"Really? Well, if you aren't using your phone under the bench you must be doing something really weird under there." I have never seen a mobile appear so fast and his face go so red. One-nil to me I think. He never did use his phone again in my class.

NOT AGAIN!

It's only 9.00pm and it's getting dark already, but we'll soon be finished. The students have thoroughly enjoyed their evening of practicals at the university and have learnt a lot. Many of the techniques were ones that we didn't have the equipment for at the college. It was well worth the agro of all the arrangements that had to be put in place to take students on a college trip, especially one in the evening. These vocational students will certainly come across the techniques they used tonight whether they go to university or find a job in a lab at the end of their A-levels.

At least it isn't cold, I think as I stand by the minibus waiting for them. Fortunately, there is plenty of lighting here at the university. I turn to our minibus driver, one of the technicians at the college.

"I can't believe it's happened again, can you?"

"Yes I can, actually."

"Really?"

"I've been driving this minibus for years now and nothing surprises me any more."

"But it was only a month ago when the last incident happened. You remember?"

"Vividly."

"It still annoys me when I think about it. I was so careful not to leave anything off the forms, and sent them out to parents well in advance. I checked I had them all back and double-checked them again. I left nothing to chance. I was quite specific, if you remember. The form stated in bold that the students would probably not be back in time to catch the school bus and that they would have to make their own arrangements to get home. None of the parents complained. None of them let me know about any issues, even though I specifically asked them to. That girl is over eighteen! She's effectively an adult. She shouldn't need her parents to sign for her permission anymore. How was I to know that her mother was so neurotic she'd actually ring up and demand that someone at the college, ie you, drive her back to her house? We're not a taxi service! To give the girl credit, she was sorry about it. But still. Crazy."

"I must admit that after the long drive back from the Isle of Wight I was tired and the thought of another hour and a half in the bus driving in all the rush-hour traffic was daunting. I felt bad for you. But you had to come with me. I can't risk taking her home on my own. Ridiculous, but it's a sign of the times."

"I know. Now, here we are again in a similar predicament, although slightly different circumstances. I mean, we're outside of work hours, aren't we? And this trip was optional. I really covered all the eventualities this time. The forms were water-tight. After the last time, I made it absolutely clear that the students have to make their own arrangements to get home and if not then they couldn't attend. It's not like not going would jeopardise their course. It's just for some extra benefit, really. I have all their home phone numbers, addresses and relevant signatures to prove it. I just don't know what went so wrong that this would happened again."

"You can't plan for the unexpected."

"You could have knocked me down with a feather when that girl came up to me in the break. 'Please Miss, I don't have a lift home,' she said. 'No problem, I have the phone number and address of your landlady. I'll ring her,' I said. I felt quite smug.

What I couldn't have foreseen, because I didn't have a crystal ball, was her saying, 'Trouble is, miss, I moved yesterday and I don't know my new address or phone number!'"

DEAD FLOWERS

The class comes running into the lab.

"Sit down, and get your practical books out quietly."

One of the students rushes up to my desk.

"Here, miss. These are what you asked me to bring today."

He lays them down in front of me. I look down at my desk and then up at him.

"Are they okay, miss?"

"Quiet, the rest of you. Go and collect a lab coat and the apparatus for the practical." I look at the lad again. "Well, can you remember our conversation from last week? I needed some dead flowers for this week."

"Yes, miss. I said my dad buys my mum fresh flowers every week and I could bring them in when they have died off."

"Yes, because I said it would be expensive to bring fresh flowers but when they are dying it would be fine."

"Trouble is, miss, Mum and Dad had a row last week and he didn't buy her any flowers. They made it up now so we only have fresh ones. I couldn't bring those in, could I?"

"No, quite right you couldn't. But you should have told me. Do you know the sort of tests we're going to carry out?"

"Miss, miss, I know," a voice comes from the back of the class.

"Be quiet, I'm not talking to you. Start writing the method in your books." I turn back to the boy. "Can you remember the tests even without the sheet?"

"Yes. We're going to put the leaves in boiling water for five minutes to extract the green chlorophyll. Then we can cut the stems open to look at the vascular bundles." He is quite chuffed with himself.

"Very good, but what about the flowers themselves?"

"We're going to collect some pollen from them." He pauses and his face changes. "Oh! We can't do the tests on these flowers, can we?"

"And why is that?"

"Because they're plastic, miss…"

LATE AGAIN

I'm sitting here racking my brain of how to solve the problem of students being late to my classes. I can vividly recall the conversation with the college inspector, who told me, "Your students must be on time for all of your classes."

"Easy for you to say. This isn't a school where the bell rings for the start of classes. The students are all over sixteen and are here because they want to be. In principle, that is," I replied.

"Yes, I realise that, but you have to find a way. Otherwise you will be downgraded for your lessons."

I had looked at him. Pompous ass, I thought. I bet you've never tried to teach these types of students. I expect yours were all grammar-school types or FE students. His voice interrupted my thoughts.

"Right, I'll leave you to mull it over. I'll be coming back again to see you. I'll expect some improvement."

"I can't wait," I said under my breath. He was right, of course. The first five minutes of any lesson are crucial. So what could I do? I had solved the problem for the A-level students. I had made a ten-minute timer out of two lemonade bottles stuck together. There was enough sand in one of them so that when you turned the timer upside-down it took ten minutes for the sand to run through into the bottle at the bottom. Very high tech, not – but it works. I give them a worksheet to complete in the time and then give them the answers and record the marks. It certainly gets them in on time.

This won't work for retake GCSE students. They have to be entertained the minute the class starts. So what can I do? Bribery would work. Not money, of course. I know, chocolates. Everyone likes chocolates, even hormonal sixteen-year-old boys.

I make a chart for each of the three classes with their names on and stick them to the wall. I buy packets of coloured dots from the stationers to stick on them. One for each class they are on time for. I also purchase a large tin of Quality Street and some bags of fun-sized chocolates. When they have acquired six dots they can get a Quality Street and when they have completed twelve they get a fun-size chocolate bar.

The students are bemused at first but it works a treat. I'll show that inspector.

However, there's one lad who is still continually late. I ask him, "Don't you like chocolates?"

"I'm not allowed to eat them, miss. I have a medical condition and I take medicine every day. I'm not allowed to eat chocolates or sweets." I'm quite cross but can't do anything about it, so he continues to be late.

One day I'm about to start the class when I feel a thud on my back and turn around abruptly. I hadn't heard the door open.

"Miss, I'm not late, well, only a couple of minutes," the same student says.

I look at him aghast. Does he realise what he has just done? He seems so pleased with himself. Although a bit shaken, I think very carefully and say, "What on Earth did you do that for?"

"I'm on time, miss. I thought you would be glad."

"I'm glad, but I'm not a pal of yours. I'm your teacher and you can't slap me on the back. No matter how well-meaning."

He seems quite taken aback.

"But I didn't mean it nastily."

"I know you didn't, but suppose I had done it to you for some reason. I would have got the sack. Instantly. I'm afraid I'll have to report this to the head of science. I'll say you're very sorry and didn't mean it."

His face falls. In that moment I think back to an incident that had happened to me in a previous school. A very nasty and rude male student had knocked one of the school's calculators onto the floor numerous times during a maths lesson, to irritate me. After several warnings from me to stop, I had gone over to him and was about to put my hand on his to stop him doing it, when he looked at me and said threateningly, "You touch me and I will have you."

I look back at my student. "Sit down and I'll speak to the head of science. I'm sure I can convince him you had no bad intentions and that you won't do it again. But you're going to have to change your ways."

"Yes, miss. I'll try."

At the end of the lesson, when they're all gone and I'm sitting in my office, I smile and think to myself. One thing is for sure. He won't be late again.

And he isn't. I'll show that inspector!

THE MAGICIAN

"Right, I think we're ready. Have you spoken to the other technician to confirm all the safety regulations for this experiment?" I ask.

"Yes," replies the technician.

"I just need you to check I have everything in place and haven't forgotten anything. I have to decide where all the students will stand so that they can all see into the fume cupboard without them getting too close."

I've thought about this experiment carefully. Sodium is highly flammable and corrosive. Although alcohol is highly flammable, it can be used safely to mop up any pieces of sodium that may fall off the tile. I can't use a water bath as such as sodium reacts violently with it, but not with alcohol. I feel sure the students would be impressed. Here they come now.

"Sit down quietly. You have ten minutes to answer the starter question. No talking."

"What are we doing today, miss?"

"Wait and see. I need everyone here before I start."

"Miss, are we having a demonstration today?"

"Yes. And I know you like the spectacular, so I think you will enjoy this one."

"Cor, is it dangerous, miss?"

"I suppose it could be, but the technician and I have made sure we have covered every eventuality."

"We love your demos, miss. We call you the Magician," One student tells me.

"Magician? That's a funny thing to say. It's not magic when I perform a demonstration."

"Oh, but we think it is. Remember the ammonium dichromate experiment when you put orange crystals into a test tube and heated it?" another student says.

"Oh, I remember that. Loads of green tea leaves shot out of the tube like magic," says another.

"Oh yeah. And I remember the black Iodine crystals you heated and all that pretty purple gas poured out of the tube," a different student says.

"That's not magic. It's a chemical reaction," I say.

"But it's magic to us. We love it."

"And what about the methane bubbles experiment? How brilliant was that? And we all had a go."

"Ooh, yes. You connected a rubber tube to the gas tap and passed the gas through a large bottle filled with diluted washing-up liquid. Copious bubbles came flying out into the air," one student starts.

"And you let us take turns setting fire to them. Some of the flames were huge. It was ace!" another student finishes.

"Stop, you're talking all at once. Yes, that last one was pretty exciting I suppose."

"So what are we doing today, miss?"

"If you've all finished the starter, gather round and I'll explain. My 'magic', as you call it. Make sure you have a pen and paper. Not too close. Can you all see?"

"Yes, miss."

"Right, I'll talk you through it. I have cut the sodium into small pieces and I'm placing a piece on the tile. I shall light the Bunsen. I'm heating the metal from above using the hottest part of a roaring Bunsen flame just beyond the blue cone. Watch carefully and write

your observations down. Okay, the metal is burning so I can remove the Bunsen."

"Wow, miss, this is brilliant."

"Look at that flame! It's getting bigger."

"Miss, miss, the container is melting."

"Wow, the alcohol has caught fire."

"It's spreading, miss."

"So it is. I must get the fire blanket and put my fire-proof gloves on. Can one of you get the technician?" I say, remembering I must try not to panic.

"This is awesome, miss."

"It may appear that way but you need to evacuate the lab," I say calmly.

"No way, miss!"

"At least go and sit down over there then."

"I've called the other technician as you asked. The fire is out. The blanket did its job, thank goodness."

"Wow, miss. That was spectacular."

"It might well have been, but that wasn't quite what was supposed to happen… What are you all laughing at?"

"You, miss. Look in the mirror. Your face looks all sooty from the smoke. From now on we will call you the dark magician."

ESCAPE

I need this cup of coffee. Hot and sweet. I don't mind teaching biology, but why do I have to use one of the main laboratories? I can teach GCSE biology just as easily in one of the small chemistry labs. A-level biology labs are so different. They have large glass containers of live insects as well as the usual plants. Greenery I can handle, but live insects, no. I'm being silly, really. There are quite a few teachers who complain about teaching in a chemistry lab, particularly if they're not science teachers. They don't like the smells, for a start. The fume cupboard can be very smelly at times, especially if we've carried out a gaseous experiment in it. And of course we have lots of bottles and jars around the room.

The lab is quiet, and I get my notes and books out for the lesson. Ah, here is the technician now.

"Do you need anything from the prep room?" she asks me.

"No, I don't think so," I reply.

The door crashes open and the students pile in.

"Settle down quietly. Get your books out. Come away from those jars."

"Miss, look at these cockroaches! Aren't they horrible?" says one student.

"Yes. And the locusts," another one joins in.

"I don't like it in here, miss," says a classmate.

"Nor do I, miss," agrees another.

"Don't worry. They can't get out. The technician always checks on them before each class comes in. Anyway, some of you do biology, don't you?" I say.

"Yes, but not in this lab. We use the smaller one without the insects."

"Right, open your books at page ten and answer the questions. You have fifteen minutes and then we can discuss the answers."

I turn to the blackboard and start writing up the homework. Soon I become aware of movement and noise behind me. It sounds as if stools are being moved. "Quieten down! You're supposed to be writing not talking," I say.

The noise gets louder. Suddenly there's a scream. I look around and one of the girls is jumping up and down.

"What on Earth is the matter?"

"Miss, there's something under the desk and it's moving," she says.

"What is it?"

"I don't know, miss."

"For goodness' sake, just bend down and look properly. It's probably a twig or the stem of a plant and you've kicked it and it's rolling around."

She lets out another scream, then says, "It's a cockroach, miss!"

"Are you sure? Let me have a look. Where?"

"There!"

I look down in horror to see a brown insect scurrying around in circles. All the students start panicking and rush to the door. Some of the boys are shouting. It is mayhem.

I shout for the technician. I hope she's in there. She comes running out to see what all the commotion is about.

"Don't open the door!" she shouts.

"What do you mean don't open the door?"

"Stand back and I'll catch him in this jam jar."

"He moves fast, doesn't he?"

"Yes, but he won't hurt you. Just sit on the chairs with your feet up. Keep calm. Screaming won't help. He's very small and certainly more frightened of you than you are of him."

"Really? Personally, I think it's the other way around."

"Got it. Funnily enough when I opened up this morning and checked all the jars and counted the insects I was sure that there were eight cockroaches, but I only counted seven. I assumed I had miscounted or that one of them was hiding in the undergrowth. Usually it's impossible for them to escape. We're very careful. Obviously, someone left the top of the jar open just far enough for one to squeeze through. This doesn't normally happen. Okay, you can carry on with the class now."

"Not likely. Class dismissed!"

THE LANDLINE PHONE

As I look at my calendar above my desk I remind myself that it's nearly Christmas. It's been a long term and a tough one. The autumn term is always the worst. With the clocks going back and the nights drawing in, it seems even longer than it really is. Still, there's just the parents' evening to get through, and then we break up for the holidays. All of my marking is up to date and I can't wait for the last day of term.

I get out my mark sheets and copies of the reports I have written and sent home to the parents. Of course, nowadays we have to be really careful what we say. After all, heaven forbid we should upset the little darlings. I think some of these parents don't realise that the advice we give is to help the students to pass their exams and get good grades, not just to vent our feelings about them. Kids are far too mollycoddled today. Some of them will find it hard to thrive in the real world.

I finish my cup of tea and go into the classroom I have been allocated for the evening. I put out the textbooks we use, examples of pieces of work completed by the students, and my large chart that shows, by means of large coloured dots, what assignments the students have completed. I hope that by looking at these they can see how much, or in some cases how little, work their son or daughter has handed in to be marked. I hope that for those who have large gaps their parents will chivvy them along to do some more work. The chart was a stroke of genius on my part as it seems to make most of them determined to complete their assignments. For this group of students the coursework accounts for fifty per cent of the marks for a vocational A level. I've found that a bit of competition in the group helps to keep them interested.

I start thinking about decorating the Christmas tree and writing my cards. I'm not up to date with these tasks but the students must come first. Suddenly there is a knock on the door and I look up to see my head of department.

"I have your first parent. Is everything ready to go?" he asks.

"Yes, I have everything." A very nice young woman comes in. "Please take a seat."

It's the one person I have been dreading. She seems a really nice lady. I can't imagine how she has such an awful son. We chat for a while and she pours out her heart to me. She appears very nervous but fortunately her son is not with her. I show her the chart.

"You can see that most of the class have dots against the pieces of work set. Unfortunately, your son doesn't since he rarely completes any coursework, and if you look at his attendance he's hardly ever here," I say.

"Yes, I know. I have tried to encourage him but he won't listen. He does just as he pleases. Nothing I say makes any difference. He just wants to hang about with his mates. I'm really worried about him."

"You know, you can ring me any time you have a problem and I'll try to sort it out. He could do the work if he put his mind to it."

"I can't do that. I haven't got a mobile phone."

"That's okay. You can ring me from your landline."

"I can't do that either."

"Why ever not?"

"The phone is in my son's bedroom. He locks the door and won't let me use the phone."

I look at her in utter disbelief.

"He won't let you in his room to use the phone?"

"No."

I turn away and think to myself. That is the most ridiculous excuse I have ever heard of. Well, there is no chance of him passing his exams then!

ACKNOWLEDGEMENTS

Thank you to my sons, Ian and Stephen. For many years, they listened uncomplainingly to endless tales of my students' exploits. They often greeted my return from work (and my general countenance) with, "Tell us what happened today, Mum!" Their early enthusiasm inspired me but, beyond that, without their help and encouragement I might never have subsequently committed some of these tales to page. I hope you enjoyed reading them and perhaps they will inspire you to record your own experiences for future generations of teaching professionals.

I would also like to thank Janine Feber and Christine Bagg for their encouragement during the preparation of this book.

Lightning Source UK Ltd.
Milton Keynes UK
UKOW01f0601030817
306604UK00001B/254/P